WITHDRAWN

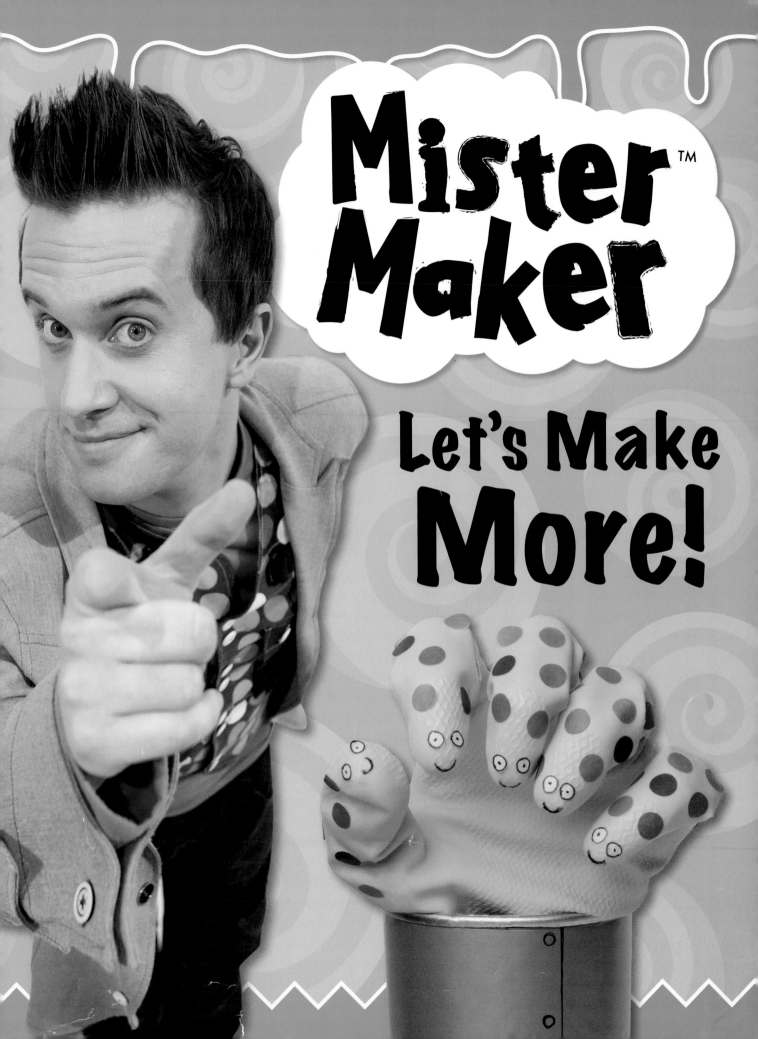

Mister Maker™

Let's Make More!

CONTENTS

It's Make Time!

3

Hello, there!
Mister Maker here.
Welcome to my second fantastic book. It's packed full of lots more great things for you to make so you'll never run out of ideas.

These pages will show you some of the things to look out for in the book. Are you ready to start? You are? Well, let's make more!

Mister Maker

Hey, look – it's those funny shapes! They'll pop up throughout the book where you least expect them!

circle

rectangle

square

triangle

When you've only got a bit of time to make something, go to the Minute Make pages where Tocky will help you along.

When you've got a bit longer, then the Medium Make pages are the place to be.

When you've got EVEN longer, go to the Massive Make pages!

Look out for the clocks at the top of the page.

Check out these crazy frames! One of these on the page means your make will look so good you'll want to frame it!

This sign means you might want an adult to help you.

This sign means you should be careful with your scissors because scissors are sharp.

FROM THE DOODLE DRAWERS

Before you start any make, you'll need some things from the Doodle Drawers such as a glue stick, scissors and a trombone... oh no, you don't need that!

pencil

paintbrush

glue stick

red paint

black felt tip pen

scissors

Cotton bud animal

Baa baa black sheep, have you any wool? This one doesn't. It's made of clay!

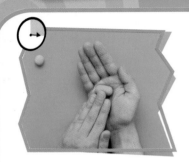

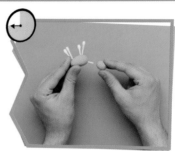

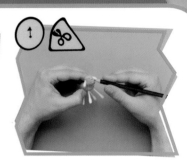

1 Roll a big ball of clay and a small ball of clay.

2 Cut two cotton buds in half. Push them into the large ball of clay to make four legs. Then cut the fluffy ends off another cotton bud, leaving the middle bit.

3 Push the middle bit of the cotton bud into the side of the big ball to make a neck. Push the smaller ball of clay on to the neck to make the head.

4 Put the two fluffy bits of cotton bud into each side of the head to make ears. Cut the fluffy end off the last cotton bud to make a tail. Now draw a face with on a pencil.

Why not use clay and cotton buds to make a whole farmyard of animals? Try this colourful chicken or what about a pig, pretty in pink?

FROM THE DOODLE DRAWERS

black and white paint

air drying clay

scissors

4 cotton buds

paintbrush

pencil

When you have more than a minute and your sheep is dry, you can paint it black and white!

Key ring charm

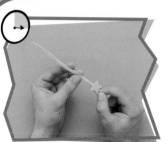

1 Thread your charm onto your pipe cleaner and twist the end of the pipe cleaner around the loop so it's secure.

2 Feed beads on to the pipe cleaner. Alternate colours to make a pretty pattern.

3 Wrap the end of the pipe cleaner round the key ring so it's secure.

You can use any colours and any charm – the possibilities are endless!

Perfect to hang on your bag, belt or lunchbox!

FROM THE DOODLE DRAWERS

pipe cleaner

charm with a loop on the back

key ring

beads

Straw rocket

FROM THE DOODLE DRAWERS

2 triangles of coloured paper

glue stick

scissors

yellow and orange tissue paper

straw

circle of paper

1 Cut your yellow and orange tissue paper into long strips to make flames. Glue these to one of the triangles of paper.

2 Turn your rocket over and glue the circle of paper onto it.

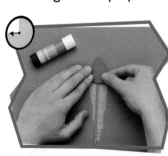

3 Stick the straw to the back of the rocket. Then stick the other triangle on top so the straw is inside the rocket.

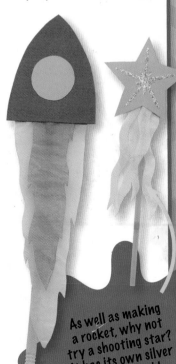

As well as making a rocket, why not try a shooting star? It has its own silver trail. Whoosh!

Can of worms

Surprise your friends with these wiggly, wriggly wormy worms!

1 Push the bottom out of your cardboard tub. You could ask an adult to help you with this bit.

2 Lay your tub at the bottom of your silver paper and make a pencil mark to show how tall it is.

3 Move the tub to the other side of the paper and make a mark there. Join up the two marks using your ruler. Then carefully cut along the line.

Or why not make disco worms with feathers and sequins? These ones are all dressed up ready to wriggle to the music!

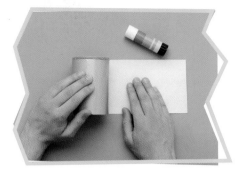

4 Put glue along the short edge of the silver paper and stick it to the edge of your tub. Roll the tub along and glue the other end of the paper down.

5 Glue the lid onto silver paper. Make small cuts in the paper, fold over the pieces and glue them down. You can cover the inside of the lid with scraps of paper.

6 Now draw a line down the side of the tub with your felt tip pen. Add some little circles to make it look like a tin.

FROM THE DOODLE DRAWERS

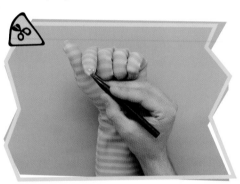

7 Draw two eyes for each worm on your white paper. Our glove has five worms so we'll need ten eyes. Cut them out. Put the glove on your hand and stick two eyes on each worm. Give each worm a smiley mouth.

8 Finally, put your rubber glove inside the tin. Put the lid on and get ready to wiggle your fingers when you take the lid off and surprise someone!

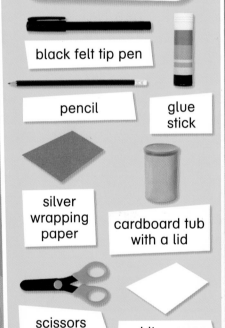

black felt tip pen

pencil

glue stick

silver wrapping paper

cardboard tub with a lid

scissors

white paper

ruler

rubber glove

Or you could try spotty worms! These are made by putting stickers onto a yellow rubber glove.

Googly pencil bug

FROM THE DOODLE DRAWERS

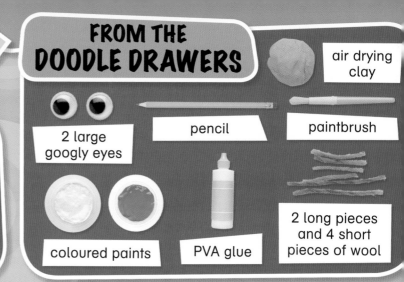

2 large googly eyes

pencil

air drying clay

paintbrush

coloured paints

PVA glue

2 long pieces and 4 short pieces of wool

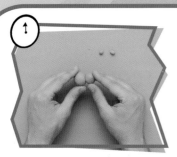

1 Take two lumps of clay, one bigger than the other. Tear two small bits off the big ball and roll them into balls. Put these to one side. Squidge the small and the large ball of clay together for the head and body.

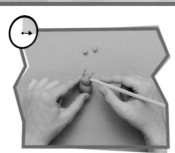

2 Tie a knot in each end of each piece of wool. Now give your pencil bug some antennae. Use a pencil to push the two of the short pieces of wool into the top of the ball.

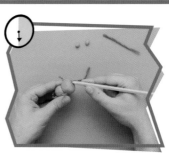

3 Use the other two short pieces of wool for the arms and the two long pieces for the legs. Push them in with the pencil, like you did before.

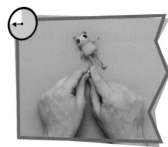

4 Stick two googly eyes on the face. Then add the two small bits of clay to the legs for feet.

5 Stick your bug onto the end of your pencil.

When your pencil bug is dry, you can paint it nice bright colours. Also, covering it in gloopy PVA glue will help it to stay stuck together.

How about making bugs in different shapes? You can even make one with lots of arms, like this four-armed creature!

Bookworm

Jazzy spinner

FROM THE DOODLE DRAWERS

glue stick

sticky tape

rubber glove

strip of card

cotton wool

scissors

2 googly eyes

1 Glue your tissue paper circle to your lid.

2 Glue all round the side of the lid. Then roll the sticky lid in plenty of glitter.

3 Glue your sequins onto the spinner. Place a ball of clay under the lid and carefully push the pencil through the lid and into the clay. Remove the clay and you're ready to spin!

Why don't you have a go at making this one with a glittery spiral? Don't get dizzy!

1 Cut two fingers off a rubber glove. Stuff each one with some cotton wool, leaving a bit of space at each end.

2 Put one end of the card inside a finger and fix it with sticky tape. Fix the other end of the card in the other finger.

FROM THE DOODLE DRAWERS

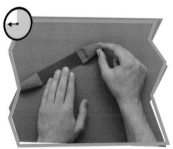

3 Turn your bookworm over and glue on two googly eyes.

You can use whatever colours you like or use circle stickers to make your worm spotty!

round lid from a cardboard cheese box

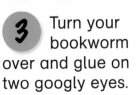

sharp pencil

ball of modelling clay

glitter

circle of tissue paper, the same size as the lid

large sequins

glue stick

Shiny fish picture

Fishing about for a good idea? Try making this fantastic fish picture!

1 Draw a blue fish on your paper. Its body is a circle. Then draw three fins and colour them in. Give it a big eye and a curvy smile. What a happy fish!

2 Take your foil and carefully cut out the fish's scales in the shape of your thumb or an upside down "U" shape. Use lots of different colours.

3 Stick the scales on to the body of the fish. Start at the back of the fish and work towards the face. Make sure you overlap the scales.

4 Now add some details with a silver pen. Don't forget to give your fish a shiny eye and some bubbles coming out of his mouth!

FROM THE DOODLE DRAWERS

dark blue felt tip pen

silver felt tip pen

blue paper

glue stick

scissors

coloured bits of foil

There's something fishy about this!

Ghostly picture

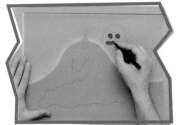

1 Using a black pastel, draw a thick line in the shape of a hill across your card. Then smudge the line with your fingers for a spooky, misty effect. It's a bit messy so wash your hands afterwards!

2 Draw a line with your pink pastel following the line of the hill. Smudge the chalk upwards to get a spooky glow!

3 Draw an old tree on top of the hill with your black chalk pastel.

4 Place the tracing paper on top of your picture and draw a ghost shape. Give it eyes and a mouth.

5 Now carefully tear your ghost out and glue it to the page.

FROM THE DOODLE DRAWERS

black felt tip pen

chalk pastels

tracing paper

pencil

glue stick

dark coloured card

Why don't you try it – if you dare!

13

FROM THE DOODLE DRAWERS

Carnival shaker

cardboard crisp tube | sticky tape

coloured paints

black felt tip pen

glue stick

paintbrush

scissors

rice

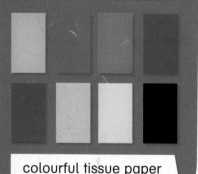

colourful tissue paper

1 Paint the outside of your crisp tube white. This makes it easier to cover with coloured paint later on. Leave it to dry.

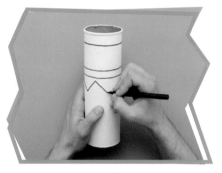

2 Draw a pattern on your tube with your felt tip pen. You could draw all sorts of shapes like circles and zig zags. Make sure you turn the tube as you draw all the way around it.

3 Now it's time to paint your shaker. Make it lovely and colourful.

4 Carefully cut up some strips of coloured tissue paper. Gather all the strips together. Twist them in the middle and fasten the bunch with sticky tape.

A fantastic carnival shaker for you to make and shake!

5 Attach the tissue paper to the lid of your tube with sticky tape. You can glue more strips to the top to make your shaker look even better.

6 Fill your tube with rice and put the lid back on. Now shake it!

Great shaker, Mister Maker!

You can make carnival shakers in all shapes and sizes, like this shorter one. You can also put different things inside them to create different sounds, like dried peas or dried macaroni pasta. With all these sounds, you can have your own carnival party!

Coin clackers

Jumbo lolly stick lizard

FROM THE DOODLE DRAWERS

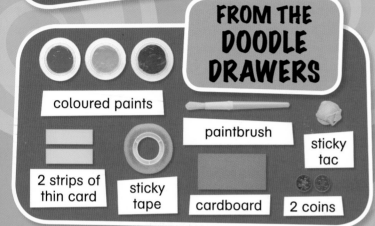

coloured paints

paintbrush

sticky tac

2 strips of thin card

sticky tape

cardboard

2 coins

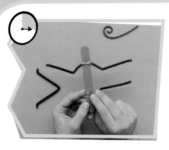

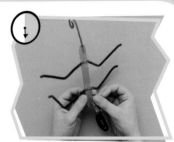

1 Bend four pipe cleaners into leg shapes and tape them onto your lolly stick. Curl and stick a red pipe cleaner to one end for a tongue.

2 Wind the last pipe cleaner round your fingers to make it curly. Tape it to the other end of the stick for a tail.

1 Fold the cardboard in half. Loop each strip of the thin card round your finger. Stick the ends down.

2 Stick each loop of card to each side of the cardboard with a piece of sticky tape.

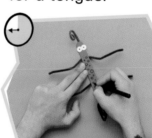

3 Use stickers for eyes and draw in the pupils. You can draw dots on the body too.

This lizard has a long tongue to lick lollies. Slurp!

3 Using sticky tac, fix the coins inside the cardboard.

When you have more than a minute, you can paint your clacker!

FROM THE DOODLE DRAWERS

6 pipe cleaners

2 white stickers

black felt tip pen

sticky tape

jumbo lolly stick

One-eyed monster

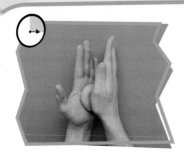
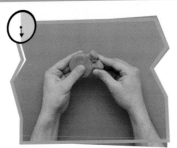
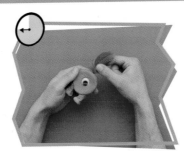

1 Break your clay into one big ball and two small balls. Squash your big ball of clay. This will be the monster's body.

2 Roll the two smaller balls of clay into sausages for the legs. Push them into the body.

3 Stick a googly eye on the front of your monster. Push a feather into the top.

4 On some card, draw some arms and carefully cut them out. Push them into your clay monster.

FROM THE DOODLE DRAWERS

scissors

large googly eye

coloured paint

card

paintbrush

feather

air drying clay

black felt tip pen

When you have more than a minute, you can paint your monster a nice bright colour.

Eye, eye!

You can make different monsters, like this blue spotty one. He has two eyes and is sitting down.

17

Joke arrow through the head

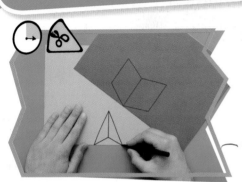

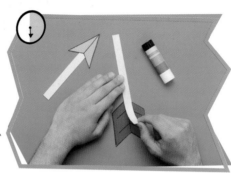

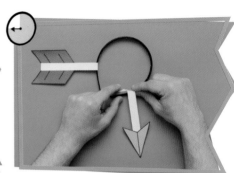

1 For the arrow head, draw two triangles on the grey card. For the end of the arrow, take the red card and draw two sloping rectangles that face each other. Carefully cut both shapes out.

2 Stick the point of your arrow to a strip of cream card. Then stick the end of the arrow to the other strip of cream card.

3 Now tape each strip to the hair band. You can fold the strip over the hair band.

It will make your friends laugh!

FROM THE DOODLE DRAWERS

red and grey card

black felt tip pen

scissors

2 thin strips of cream card

sticky tape

glue stick

hair band

Look at these beautiful bunches with pink hair bands that you could make. Or what about cow horns and cow ears? Very a-moo-sing!

Fancy dress headdress

Nothing to wear for a fancy dress party? Here's a solution. Just use your head!

1 First, make sure your strip of card fits around your head. You could ask an adult to help you. Lay your feathers along your strip of card. Stick them in place with sticky tape.

2 Turn your strip of card over and glue a big jewel in the middle. Now add stickers and jewels beside it.

3 Finally, stick the ends of the card together with sticky tape. Time to wear it!

FROM THE DOODLE DRAWERS

strip of card that fits around your head

glue stick

sticky tape

feathers

stickers

plastic jewels

If you've got more than a minute, why not try this one too? As well as feathers, it has twigs and leaves!

Picture of a dinosaur skeleton

Dinosaurs might be extinct, but this one appears like magic! The wax crayon dinosaur shows through the wet paint.

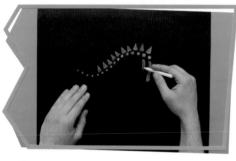

1 Before you draw your dinosaur on white paper, practise with a white crayon on dark paper. Make the spine by drawing a line of dots that gets bigger towards the head.

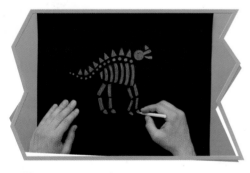

2 Draw a line of triangles for the dinosaur's spikes. Add curved lines to make the ribs. The ribs get shorter as they get closer to the tail.

3 Add a head with a horn and a mouth. Draw two sausages and a triangle in a line for each of the dinosaur's four legs.

4 Now you've practised, draw the dinosaur in the same way on the white paper. It'll seem a bit strange but all will be revealed!

5 Add some red paint to one of the cups of water. Stir the mixture, which should be nice and runny. Do exactly the same with the orange and the pink paint.

6 Paint coloured stripes across the white paper until you reach the bottom of the page. It looks great if the colours blend together. Your dinosaur will appear, bit by bit!

FROM THE DOODLE DRAWERS

three cups with a little water

dark paper

white paper

paintbrush

white wax crayon

coloured paints

Do you think he saur-us?!

21

Pirate-shaped treasure chest

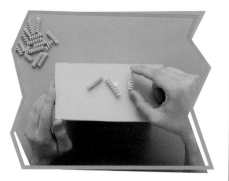

1 First cover your box in white paint. When it is dry, mix some white and brown paint and use it to colour your box light brown.

2 When the paint is dry, add the hair. To do this, dip each pasta swirl in glue and stick them all on top of the box.

What does every pirate need? A pirate-shaped chest to keep his treasure safe!

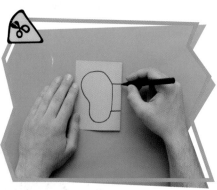

3 Fold the brown paper in half. Draw a rectangle and then an ear shape near the open edge of the fold. Add some ear details and carefully cut it out. Unfold the paper to give you two ear shapes.

FROM THE DOODLE DRAWERS

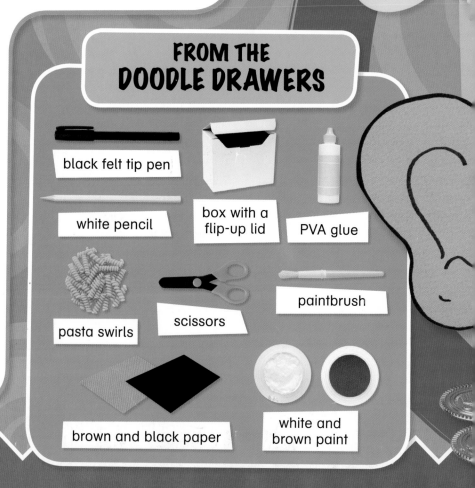

black felt tip pen

white pencil

box with a flip-up lid

PVA glue

pasta swirls

scissors

paintbrush

brown and black paper

white and brown paint

4 Fold along the rectangle to make a flap. Glue each ear to each side of your box.

5 Draw a pirate face on the front of your box. Don't forget an eye patch!

6 Fold a piece of black paper in half. Draw a hat with your white pencil. Make sure that the top of the hat touches the fold. Carefully cut it out but do not cut along the fold.

7 Paint his eye and teeth white. You can even paint a white skull and crossbones on the hat.

8 When the pirate hat is dry, open it and glue it on top of his pasta hair.

Shiver me timbers!

Torn paper picture

What tall skyscrapers! How many buildings can you see in the city?

1 Draw two rectangles on light grey paper. Draw another with a pointy top and one with a curved roof. Tear all the shapes out by placing a ruler along each pencil line and ripping the paper against it.

2 Repeat this on dark grey paper using a white pencil, making your buildings smaller this time. Do it again on black paper. This time make your buildings even smaller and make sure they are joined up at the bottom of the page. Tear everything out.

3 Now glue all your buildings to a piece of yellow paper. Put your biggest buildings at the back and your smallest buildings at the front.

4 Finally, tear some newspaper into rectangles and squares for windows and doors. Glue them onto your buildings and add some details with a felt tip pen.

FROM THE DOODLE DRAWERS

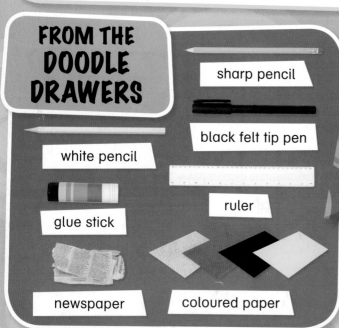

sharp pencil

black felt tip pen

white pencil

ruler

glue stick

newspaper

coloured paper

It's a fabulous torn paper city!

Tin foil treasure

 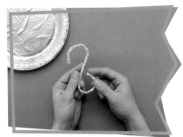  

1 Using a paintbrush, cover your plate with glue and then a big piece of tin foil. Make sure you cover both sides of the plate.

2 Take three strips of tin foil and twist them into sausage shapes. Next bend them into curly shapes. Glue these onto your plate.

3 Twist a shorter strip of tin foil and then curl it into a ring shape. Stick this onto the middle of your plate.

4 Fold or scrunch up sweet wrappers so they look like gems. Glue them onto your plate in a pretty pattern.

You can turn anything you like into treasure! What about a gorgeous goblet, made out of a plastic beaker?

FROM THE DOODLE DRAWERS

paper plate

tin foil

shiny sweet wrappers

paintbrush

PVA glue

To find ye the treasure, one thing is clear, you'll need lots of tin foil for this great idea!

25

Firefly

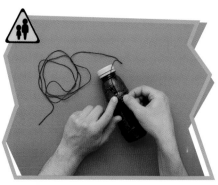

There's no need to be afraid of the dark with this glowing firefly. He'll light the place up!

FROM THE DOODLE DRAWERS

black felt tip pen

scissors

empty plastic bottle

sticky tape

string

white and black craft foam

silver felt tip pen

glow stick

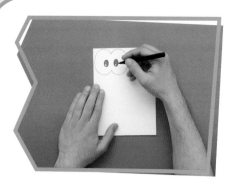

1 Draw two eyes on some white craft foam with your black pen. Make sure they are joined together in one piece. Add some dots to the middle of the eyes.

2 Draw two wings on more white craft foam. Carefully cut out the eyes and the wings.

3 Draw some antennae on black craft foam with a silver pen or a white pencil. Carefully cut them out.

4 Take a long piece of string and wrap it around your plastic bottle. Fix it tightly with a knot. Use sticky tape to fix the knot to the bottle.

4 Fix the antennae to the front of the bottle top using sticky tape.

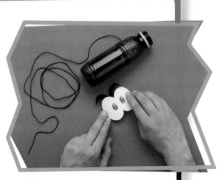

5 Stick the eyes on top of the antennae using a loop of sticky tape. Then stick your wings to the bottle.

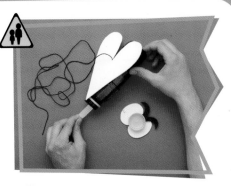

6 Bend your glow stick until you hear it snap. Give it a shake and it glows! Put it inside the bottle and put the lid back on. Hang it up and you have a glowing firefly!

It glows in the dark!

You're a bright spark, Mister Maker!

Splatter space picture

Make sure you do all this on some old newspaper as it can get messy!

1 Dip an old toothbrush in the white paint mixture. To create the sky, scrape the cardboard across the toothbrush over your black paper. Move the card towards you or you'll splatter yourself!

2 When the paint is dry, rip out some crater shapes from your brown paper. Place them on your picture and draw some detail with a pen.

3 Splatter the red and orange paper with the red and yellow paint mixtures. When it's dry, draw some planets. You could draw around a roll of sticky tape. Cut them all out.

4 Draw an alien on your white paper, paint him crazy colours and carefully cut him out. When the paint is dry, add some detail in pen. Stick down your alien, craters and planets.

It's out of this world!

FROM THE DOODLE DRAWERS

black, brown, red, orange and white paper

white, red and yellow paint mixed with a little water

green and pink paint

cardboard

sticky tape

glue stick

scissors

black felt tip pen

old toothbrush

paintbrush

Bookend secret safe

 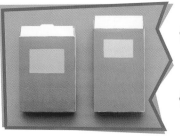  

1 Cover both your boxes, including the flaps, in white paint. This makes it easier to cover in coloured paint later. Now wait for the paint to dry.

2 Paint the back, the front and one long side of each box with coloured paint. Leave the other sides white. When your boxes are dry, paint pale rectangles on the front.

3 Add in detail with a pen. If you put lines on all the white edges, they will look like pages. Draw rectangles on the spine and on the front to look like a real book.

4 Put some pebbles in each box to weigh them down. Now you can put in whatever you want. Once they're shut, no one will know what's inside – except you!

FROM THE DOODLE DRAWERS

- black felt tip pen
- 2 cardboard cereal boxes
- paintbrush
- coloured paints
- pebbles

How many rectangles can you see?

29

MINUTE MAKES

Wobbly clown

Fancy clowning around? Try making these wibbly, wobbly creatures. They rock!

1 Open your plastic egg and put the ball of modelling clay inside so that the egg wobbles when you stand it up.

2 Glue two googly eyes on your egg. Put plenty of glue on your pom-pom and stick it on the egg for a nose.

3 Draw a smiley mouth on your white paper. Carefully cut it out and glue it onto your egg.

4 Scrunch two pieces of tissue paper up to make some crazy hair. Stick each piece on either side of the egg.

FROM THE DOODLE DRAWERS

red felt tip pen

white paper

scissors

glue stick

2 googly eyes

small pom-pom

2 pieces of tissue paper

ball of modelling clay

plastic egg that opens in two halves

How about making a pig using a pink egg with a paper snout? Or you could make a rockin' elephant with a paper trunk and ears!

Surprise spring bug

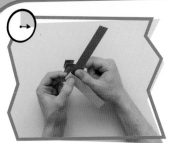

1 Glue the two strips of card in an "L" shape. Fold one strip over and then the other. Continue until you have a spring.

2 Stick two googly eyes onto your pom-pom. Then glue your bug onto one end of the spring.

3 Glue the spring into the pot. When someone opens the pot, the bug will spring out and surprise them!

FROM THE DOODLE DRAWERS

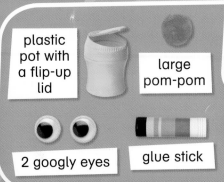

plastic pot with a flip-up lid

large pom-pom

2 googly eyes

glue stick

2 strips of card

Paper pet fish

FROM THE DOODLE DRAWERS

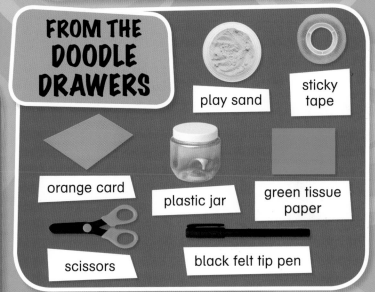

play sand

sticky tape

orange card

plastic jar

green tissue paper

scissors

black felt tip pen

1 Put some play sand in your plastic jar so that it covers the bottom of the pot.

2 Draw a fish on your card. Cut it out. Add a long loop of sticky tape to the back of the fish and stick it into the pot.

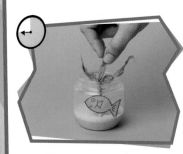

3 Tear up some tissue paper for seaweed. Twist it, bunch it together and push it into the sand.

Easy winter picture

Brr! It's cold outside! Luckily you can stay in the warm to make this snowy scene.

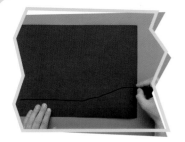   

1 Draw a line for the ground onto your paper using a black felt tip pen.

2 Draw a house outline. Then add a fence and a leafy tree.

3 Now paint your house and garden and let it dry.

4 Use your paintbrush to dab white paint anywhere that snow would fall, like the roof, the top of the fence and the grass. You could even add some snowflakes falling from the sky!

Look! It's snowing!

FROM THE DOODLE DRAWERS

paintbrush

dark blue paper

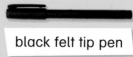

black felt tip pen

coloured paints

How many squares can you see?

Bubble painting

Make sure you wear an apron for this one as it can get a bit messy!

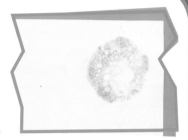

1 Put some washing-up liquid into a cup. Add some PVA glue, water and blue paint. Stir the mixture with a straw. Do the same with the other two colours of paint.

2 Using a straw, blow into the mixture until the bubbles rise above the cup. Be careful not to suck!

3 Gently lay a sheet of white paper on top of the cup.

4 The bubble of paint makes a print on the paper.

How about making bubbly wrapping paper or a bubbly birthday card?

5 Do the same with your other colours until you have made a fantastic pattern.

FROM THE DOODLE DRAWERS

white paper

water

coloured paints

washing-up liquid

3 cups

straw

PVA glue

Super sticky picture

You can arrange and rearrange these sticky scouring pads how you like. The sky's the limit!

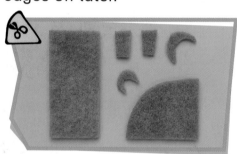

1 Cover your cardboard in glue using a paintbrush. Stick on four dark scouring pads. If they are bigger than the card, you can cut the edges off later.

2 From a red scouring pad cut a rectangle for the rocket's body and two smaller rectangles for boosters. Cut a quarter circle for the planet and two crescents for its craters.

3 Take a yellow pad and cut out a triangle for the top of the rocket, a rectangle for the rocket's base and a thin strip for the planet's ring.

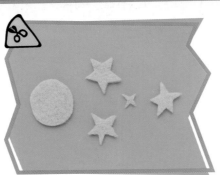

4 From a blue scouring pad, cut out some triangles for the rocket's wings and some small circles for the windows. What a lot of cutting!

5 Now you just need a moon and some stars. Cut all of these out of a yellow or white scouring pad.

6 Now put all your shapes on the sticky board. You can change them and stick the pieces on top of each other in different ways. You could even cut out new shapes.

FROM THE DOODLE DRAWERS

coloured kitchen scouring pads

PVA glue

cardboard

paintbrush

scissors

Whoosh! What a fantastic rocket. Lift-off!

FROM THE DOODLE DRAWERS

air drying clay

PVA glue

rolling pin

sharp pencil

plastic tray

plastic jar

paintbrush

green and black paint

What a handy way to keep your treasures safe!

Gruesome jar

A great but gruesome jar to protect all your favourite bits and pieces!

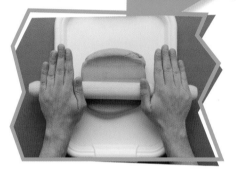

1 On an old tray, roll out a ball of air drying clay using a rolling pin. Roll out enough clay so you can fit your whole hand on top of it.

2 Put your hand on the clay and, pushing your pencil in the clay, draw a shape that is a bit bigger than your hand so that it looks like a monster's hand!

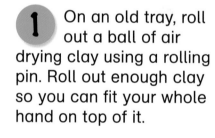

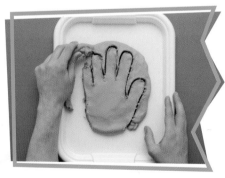

3 Peel away the left-over clay from around the hand. Be careful not to break off any of the fingers!

4 Bend the fingers over the lid of the jar. You could use a ball of tissue paper to support the hand while it dries.

5 Squeeze the ends of the fingers to make long nails. Add bits of clay to make your hand extra old and wrinkly!

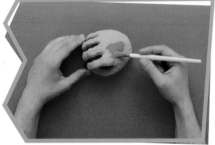

6 Lift the hand off the lid and leave it to dry. Paint it green with black fingernails.

7 Glue the hand on the lid and you're done! Painting PVA glue over the hand will make it extra strong.

Jazzy pot

Silly springy eyes

FROM THE DOODLE DRAWERS

- paintbrush
- air drying clay
- plastic tray
- PVA glue
- sequins and beads
- rolling pin
- plastic plant pot

1 Take a strip of card of each colour and fold one over one way and then the other over the other way until you have a spring. Do the same with the other two strips.

2 Put the stickers on your circles of card and draw in some pupils. Glue one circle of card onto the end of each spring.

3 Make two loops of sticky tape and stick one spring onto each eye of the sunglasses.

FROM THE DOODLE DRAWERS

4 strips of card

2 circles of card

glue stick

2 white stickers

sticky tape

old sunglasses

black felt tip pen

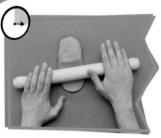
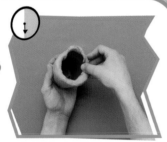

1 Roll out your clay into a flat sausage shape using a rolling pin.

2 Cover your plant pot in the rolled-out clay. Make sure you push the clay down over the top of the pot.

3 Fill your tray with sequins and beads. Roll your pot in them, making sure plenty of them stick.

When your pot is dry and you've got more than a minute, cover it in PVA glue. This will keep all the bits in place.

Pine cone creature

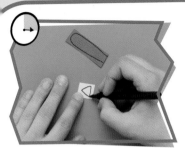

1 On a piece of pink card, draw a bird's head with a long neck. On a piece of yellow card, draw a triangle for a beak.

2 Carefully cut the head and the beak out. Now glue the beak onto the head using the glue stick.

3 Stick two googly eyes onto your head. Put some PVA glue on the bottom of the neck and stick it in the pine cone.

4 Now give your bird some feathers. Glue each feather into the pine cone so they're secure.

FROM THE DOODLE DRAWERS

pink and yellow card

black felt tip pen

PVA glue

glue stick

feathers

pine cone

scissors

2 googly eyes

It's a pine cone turkey!

Why not make a dog like me, with pipe cleaners? Woof!

39

Bubble wrap octopus

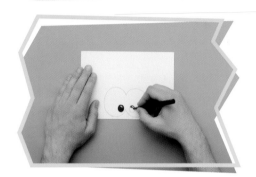

1 With a pencil, draw two circles on white paper. To make sure they are the same size, you could draw round a roll of sticky tape. Add pupils with a felt tip pen.

2 On your yellow paper, draw some circles in different sizes. Carefully cut out all your circles, including the eyes.

3 Using a glue stick, attach the circles and eyes on to your paper plate. Draw on a mouth with a felt tip pen.

FROM THE DOODLE DRAWERS

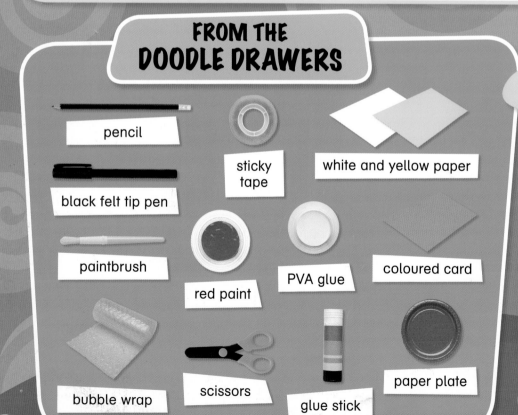

pencil

sticky tape

white and yellow paper

black felt tip pen

paintbrush

PVA glue

coloured card

red paint

bubble wrap

scissors

glue stick

paper plate

How many circles can you see?

4 Make a gloopy mixture of half PVA glue and half red paint. Stir it with your paintbrush and paint the bubbly side of your bubble wrap.

5 When the paint is dry, cut out eight wiggly strips for tentacles. They don't all have to be the same length.

6 Turn the legs over so they are bubble-side down. Stick each tentacle onto the back of the plate with sticky tape.

7 To finish, stick your octopus on to a piece of coloured card.

FROM THE DOODLE DRAWERS

pencil

paper

glitter

paintbrush

coloured paints

plastic fork

sequins and beads

All this painting is making me hungry!

Gooey cake picture

No flour... no eggs... the recipe for this cake is lots of gooey paint!

1 Start off by drawing the outline of a cake with sponge layers on your paper.

2 Paint every other cake layer with thick paint. The blank ones will be for the delicious filling.

3 Use a plastic fork to make criss-cross patterns in the thick paint. Sprinkle glitter on the paint and leave it to dry.

4 Paint the filling with a different colour. Paint slightly over the layers to make it look gooey! Sprinkle sequins and beads onto the wet paint. Leave it to dry.

5 For the icing on top of the cake, use pink paint and sprinkle beads and sequins on it. Wait for it all to dry.

6 For the cream topping, add blobs of thick white paint on top of the icing. Dot pink paint at the top and swirl it through with the end of your fork.

This cake looks good but it won't taste good – it's just a piece of brilliant art!

What a fantastically gooey cake!

Leaf print hedgehog picture

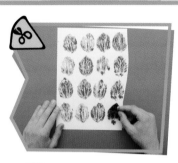

1 On your green paper, paint a grey triangle for the hedgehog's snout and then blend some brown paint into it. Draw some fork shapes for the feet.

2 Put a leaf down so that its bumpy side is facing up. Cover the leaf in brown paint and place it painted-side down on some white paper.

3 Peel the leaf off and you've got a leaf print! Do this until you've filled the paper with prints. Wait for them to dry. Carefully cut out each leaf.

4 Glue each leaf onto your picture to make the hedgehog's body. Make sure all the leaves are pointing outwards. Add a nose and two eyes with black pen.

FROM THE DOODLE DRAWERS

glue stick

grey and brown paint

green and white paper

black felt tip pen

leaves

scissors

paintbrush

It's Harry the Hedgehog, printed with the leaves he loves to play in!

Try branching out with this brilliant stag! It's made by painting a stag's body and printing antlers with curvy leaves.

Crazy dancing skeleton

It's best to lay each section out before you stick them down!

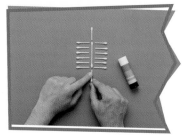

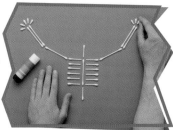

1 Cut some cotton buds in half. Take some more and cut off the fluffy ends. Now you have a pile of whole buds, a pile of half buds and a pile of short fluffy ends.

2 Glue a long bud in the centre of your paper. Now stick a half bud above it and a half bud below it. Stick half buds either side of this line for the rib cage.

3 For each waving arm you will need to stick down three long cotton buds and five fluffy ends for fingers.

4 Make a triangle shape under the rib cage with one long bud and two half buds. For each leg stick down three long buds, three half buds and five fluffy ends.

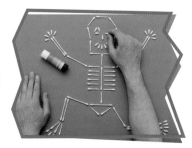

5 All he needs now is a head. Stick down nine half buds for his head and twelve fluffy ends for his eyes, nose and mouth.

It's your new buddy, Bones the skeleton!

FROM THE DOODLE DRAWERS

lots of cotton buds

dark paper

scissors

glue stick

How many triangles can you see?

Submarine pencil case

Splish splosh! Dive into this idea! It's a super submarine that's also a pencil case!

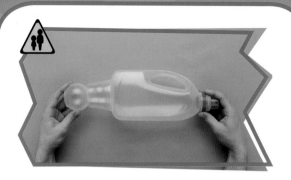

1 Ask an adult to help you clean and dry out all your plastic containers. Your fabric conditioner bottle is the main body of the submarine. Put the pot, without its lid, at one end. Place the washing ball after the pot.

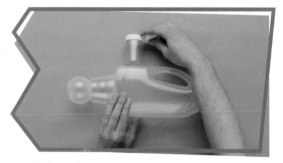

2 Put the plastic bottle with the flip up lid on the top of the fabric conditioner bottle to make a periscope.

3 Put the pot lid on the bottom of the conditioner bottle so your pencil case can stand up.

FROM THE DOODLE DRAWERS

paintbrushes

yellow tissue paper

washing ball with a flat bottom

small plastic bottle with a flip-up lid

pot with a lid

blue and red paint

PVA glue

 masking tape

black felt tip pen

plastic fabric conditioner bottle with a wide neck and lid

4 Stick it all together with masking tape. Make sure you don't put any tape over the end of the washing ball – that's where you'll put your pencil sharpeners and rubbers.

5 Now you can cover everything with a layer of PVA glue and coloured tissue paper. Add as many layers as you like and leave it to dry.

6 When it's dry you can paint on some porthole windows and some stripes.

Life beneath the waves, in a yellow submarine!

7 Now cover the plastic lids with a mix of half PVA glue and half blue paint. When it's dry, add some details to your submarine with a felt tip pen.

You can unscrew the lid and put your pencils inside. Smaller things like rubbers can go in the washing ball. Ship-shape!

My making time's over, but yours is just beginning!

Time to go! But you can come back whenever you like!

DK

LONDON, NEW YORK, MELBOURNE, MUNICH AND DELHI

Project Editor Elizabeth Dowsett
Project Art Editor Julie Thompson
Managing Editor Catherine Saunders
Art Director Lisa Lanzarini
Publishing Manager Simon Beecroft
Category Publisher Alex Allan
Production Editor Sean Daly
Production Controller Nick Seston

Photography by Andy Crawford

First published in Great Britain in 2009
by Dorling Kindersley Limited,
80 Strand, London, WC2R 0RL

Mister Maker ™ & © 2009 The Foundation.
Licensed by RDF Rights.

Page design copyright © 2009 Dorling Kindersley Limited
A Penguin Company

2 4 6 8 10 9 7 5 3 1
MD586 – 07/09

A CIP catalogue record for this book is available
from the British Library

ISBN: 978-1-40534-151-6

Colour reproduction by Media Development and Printing Ltd, UK
Printed and bound in China by L-Rex

DK would like to thank: Rachel Barke, Alison Carney, Tamsin
McArdle, Demi Charalambous, Hannah Boehm and Ailsa Smeaton
at RDF Rights; Sanna King and Suzie Harrison for craft-making;
Rhys Thomas for hand-modelling; Laura Gilbert for proof-reading
and Andy Crawford for the fabulous photography.

Discover more at
www.dk.com